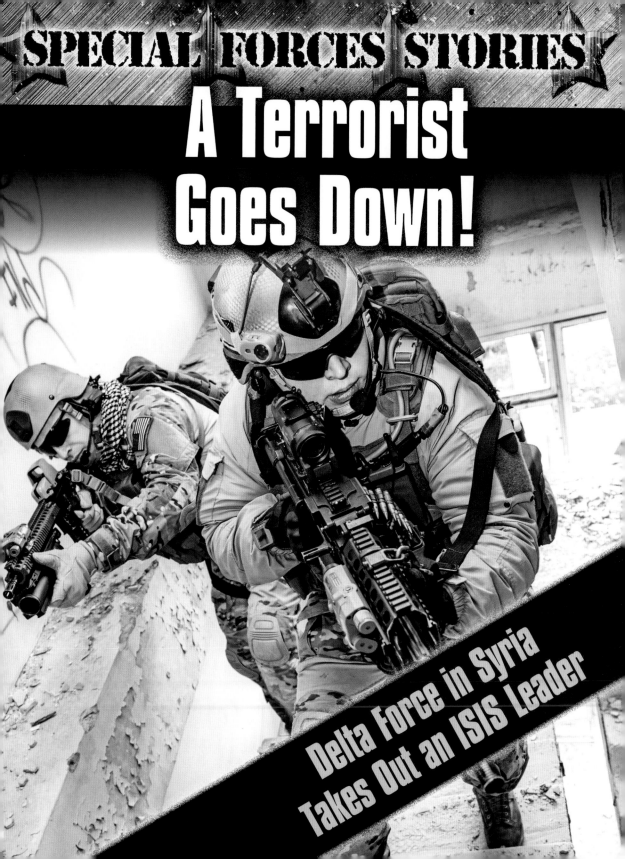

SPECIAL FORCES STORIES

A Terrorist Goes Down!

Delta Force in Syria Takes Out an ISIS Leader

SPECIAL FORCES STORIES

Captured!
Bringing in 9/11 Mastermind Khalid Sheikh Mohammed

Going After Sparky!
Pararescue Jumpers Bring Vietnam War Pilot Home

Rescue from an ISIS Prison!
Delta Force in Iraq During the War on Terror

Saving Private Lynch!
A Rescue Story from Operation Iraqi Freedom

Storming the Somali Pirates!
Navy SEALs Save Hostages

Take Out Bin Laden!
Navy SEALs Hit the Most Wanted Man

A Terrorist Goes Down!
Delta Forces in Syria Take Out an ISIS Leader

World War II Prison Breakout!
Army Rangers Make Their Mark

A Terrorist Goes Down!

Delta Force in Syria Takes Out an ISIS Leader

By John Perritano

Mason Crest

Mason Crest
450 Parkway Drive, Suite D
Broomall, PA 19008
www.masoncrest.com

© 2019 by Mason Crest, an imprint of National Highlights, Inc.

Printed and bound in the United States of America.

Series ISBN: 978-1-4222-4077-9
Hardback ISBN: 978-1-4222-4084-7
EBook ISBN: 978-1-4222-7717-1

First printing
1 3 5 7 9 8 6 4 2

Produced by Shoreline Publishing Group LLC
Editorial Director: James Buckley Jr.
Designer: Bill Madrid
Production: Sandy Gordon
www.shorelinepublishing.com
Cover photograph by Oleg Zabielin/Alamy Stock Photo.

Library of Congress Cataloging-in-Publication Data
Names: Perritano, John, author.
Title: A terrorist goes down! : Delta Forces in Syria take out an ISIS leader / by John Perritano.
Description: Broomall, PA : Mason Crest, [2018] | Series: Special forces stories | Includes index.
Identifiers: LCCN 2017053435| ISBN 9781422240847 (hardback) | ISBN 9781422240779 (series) | ISBN 9781422277171 (ebook)
Subjects: LCSH: United States. Army. Delta Force--Juvenile literature. | United States. Army--Commando troops--Juvenile literature. | IS (Organization)--Juvenile literature. | Special operations (Military science)--Syria--Juvenile literature. | Terrorism--Syria--Juvenile literature. | Terrorism--Prevention--Juvenile literature. | War on Terrorism, 2001-2009--Juvenile literature.
Classification: LCC UA34.S64 P46 2019 | DDC 956.9104/238--dc23 LC record available at https://lccn.loc.gov/2017053435

QR Codes disclaimer:

CONTENTS

Key Icons to Look For

 Words to Understand: These words with their easy-to-understand definitions will increase the reader's understanding of the text, while building vocabulary skills.

 Sidebars: This boxed material within the main text allows readers to build knowledge, gain insights, explore possibilities, and broaden their perspectives by weaving together additional information to provide realistic and holistic perspectives.

 Educational Videos: Readers can view videos by scanning our QR codes, providing them with additional educational content to supplement the text. Examples include news coverage, moments in history, speeches, iconic moments, and much more!

 Text-Dependent Questions: These questions send the reader back to the text for more careful attention to the evidence presented here.

 Research Projects: Readers are pointed toward areas of further inquiry connected to each chapter. Suggestions are provided for projects that encourage deeper research and analysis.

 Series Glossary of Key Terms: This back-of-the-book glossary contains terminology used throughout this series. Words found here increase the reader's ability to read and comprehend higher-level books and articles in this field.

MISSION BRIEFING

I t seems as if they came out of nowhere. It's June 2014, and a terrorist group based in Iraq blitzes across Syria and Iraq to the gates of Baghdad. They drive in tan Toyota trucks with a black flag waving. The terrorists capture large portions of eastern Syria, and northern and western Iraq.

The Iraq War, which had begun in 2003 with a US-led invasion, is supposed to be over. But now a new battle in this volatile region is underway. Hundreds of thousands of people who supported Iraq's brutal dictator, Saddam Hussein, are angry. Saddam is dead and they have no jobs. They are penniless. Many had been imprisoned by the Americans, and became **radicalized**. They are filled with hate. Hate for the United States and its allies. Hate for the Western world. Hate for those who are not like them. They are Muslims, but they

Words To Understand

destabilized cause unrest

heretic a person who has differences with a religious teaching

jihadist a person who believes in a holy war

morphed changed

occupation the action of being conquered by a military force

radicalized adopted a radical position on a political or social issue

sectarian relating to different groups

Armed pickup trucks flying the black ISIS flag quickly became familiar sights on TV news in the 2000s.

do not believe in peace as Muslims do. They want to push their radical and violent brand of Islam on the world.

They move into Syria and meet up with others who share their views. They call themselves the Islamic State of Iraq and Syria—ISIS, for short. Its founder is a man named Abu Musab al-Zarqawi. He is a one-time petty criminal and a bloodthirsty fanatic. He moved to Iraq from his native Jordan to fight the Americans and their allies during the Iraq War. He died in 2006 when US warplanes attacked his lair. Zarqawi is dead, but ISIS lives on.

7

Residents of Mosul, Iraq, fought to prevent their home city from being overrun by ISIS forces.

As ISIS marches across the desert toward Baghdad, the Iraqi army tries to stop the group. It fails. Soldiers run away in retreat. ISIS militants seize billions of dollars in weapons and equipment left behind by the US military. The terrorists aren't afraid to die. That's the least of their worries. They only want to destroy and kill.

The world watches in horror as ISIS fighters seize the Iraqi cities of Mosul, Tikrit, Fallujah, and Ramadi. As they move through these cities, ISIS beheads their enemies and foreign journalists. They kidnap women and use them as slaves. They stone others to death. All the while they videotape their actions and broadcast them around the world. They hope to rally others to their cause.

ISIS' new leader, Abu Bakr al-Baghdadi, declares a religious caliphate, or kingdom, in the territory ISIS holds in Syria and Iraq. He appoints himself the unquestionable ruler. He tells the world's 1.8 billion Muslims to answer only to him. He wants them to move to Iraq and Syria and become soldiers. Some do.

In no time, ISIS becomes the most powerful terrorist organization in the world. It is much strong than al-Qaeda, the group responsible for the September 11, 2001, attacks on New York and Washington, DC.

As ISIS extends its reach into Iraq and Syria, it uses captured oil to finance its deadly reign of terror. Some experts suggest the group is pumping up to 40,000 barrels of crude oil a day from the energy-rich fields. The group illegally sells the oil for between $20 and $45 a barrel, earning ISIS, on average, $1.5 million a day.

At the head of this multi-million-dollar enterprise is Abu Sayyaf. No one really knows who he is. He is mostly invisible, a terrorist without a face. The

The Many Names of ISIS

ISIS, or the Islamic State of Iraq and Syria, goes by many names. They include:

ISIL: Islamic State of Iraq and the Levant (Greater Syria). President Obama and other officials used this name to describe the group.

IS: ISIS changed its name to Islamic State to showcase its global strategy was not limited to Syria and Iraq.

Daesh: The Arabic abbreviation for the group.

most dangerous kind. Yet, he is very important. He acts as if he is running a company. He has a lot of information. He knows a lot of people. He knows where the money is. He knows where it goes. He has access to information—information the Americans need to defeat ISIS.

That knowledge has put a target on Sayyaf's back. To stop ISIS, the United States decides to go after its source of money—its oil, its black gold. The US also goes after Sayyaf himself. It will be the job of an elite group of US Army commandos—Delta Force—to find Sayyaf and deliver a major blow to ISIS and its financial network.

This is a photo of a man believed to be Abu Sayyaf, the man Delta Force was tasked to bring to justice.

US forces passed beneath huge statues of crossed swords as they moved into Iraq in 2003.

The Iraq War

ISIS did indeed seem to come out of nowhere in 2014. Yet, its seeds as a terrorist organization were planted more than 10 years before when the United States invaded Iraq. On March 19, 2003, the United States, Great Britain, and several other countries, went to war to oust Iraqi dictator Saddam Hussein.

At that time, President George W. Bush claimed—wrongly, it would turn out—that Saddam was secretly producing weapons of mass destruction (WMD). Bush and others said Iraq had chemical and biological weapons. Bush also feared Hussein and Iraq were well on their way to building the most powerful WMD of all—a nuclear weapon.

In late December 2003, President George W. Bush addressed the nation to report the capture of Saddam Hussein.

In the run-up to war, the Bush administration repeatedly overstated the threat Iraq posed to the United States and the world. Officials also said that Hussein was somehow involved in the September 11 terrorist attacks. Hussein, a US Senate Intelligence Committee report would later conclude, was never involved.

Still, the invasion took place. American, British, and other troops stormed into the ancient land and defeated Hussein's army. In the end, the United States captured Saddam. He was hiding in a "spider's hole" underground.

The new Iraqi government put Hussein on trial. A court found him guilty and hanged him. No one ever found any weapons of mass destruction. Despite Saddam Hussein's death and the **occupation** of Iraq by US forces, the Iraq War **destabilized** an already unstable region.

The Birth of ISIS

At the time, US Vice President Richard Cheney boasted that the Iraqi people would welcome the Americans as "liberators," or saviors. Nothing of the sort happened. Instead, after major combat operations were supposedly over, and after President Bush proclaimed, "mission accomplished," the United States and its allies hunkered down in what would become a deadly occupation.

Shiite vs. Sunni

Shia and Sunnis are two different groups of Muslims that split off from one another centuries ago when the Prophet Muhammad died in 632. At that time, there was great controversy over who would be Muhammad's successor. The Shiites believed that the Prophet's heir should come from Muhammad's family. The Sunnis believed the new Muslim leader should be the person who was the best leader.

Tensions between both sides often erupted in conflict over the decades. The Shiites tended to be the minority and lived in the poorest sections of Muslim society in countries governed by Sunnis. The Shiites viewed themselves as being oppressed and discriminated against. Sunni extremists consider the Shia heretics. The division within Islam continues to play a huge part in Mideast politics today.

Foreign terrorists flooded into Iraq to fight the Americans and their Iraqi allies. Moreover, a bloody **sectarian** war between Sunni and Shia Muslims drove millions from their homes. The civil war tossed the region into even more chaos.

At that time, ISIS was not known as ISIS. Instead, it was called al-Qaeda in Iraq. Under the command of Zarqawi, the group began its bloodletting by blowing up the United Nations headquarters in Baghdad in August 2003. They also killed innocent Iraqis, Americans, and others.

A surge of US troops put a lid on the violence for a moment. Then, under President Barack Obama, the US began to withdraw troops from the country.

US forces aimed artillery shells at entrenched Iraqi forces during the 2003 action.

This explosion came from an airstrike at a suspected hideout for ISIS forces near Fallujah, Iraq.

The drawdown created an opening that made it easier for terrorist organizations to gain power and territory.

Al-Qaeda in Iraq **morphed** into ISIS and began to extend its terror campaign throughout the region. They used social media to recruit fighters and to spread **jihadist** doctrine. They were brutal killers. They murdered journalists, aid workers, and others. The world had never seen anything like it.

Oil and Terror

Terrorism is a costly business. Weapons must be bought. Employee salaries must be paid. Travel. Vehicles. Food. Such things are not cheap. All cost

The nation of Iraq is dotted with oil fields and the oil is piped onto tankers from docks such as this one.

money. The leaders of ISIS knew that if they wanted to spread their beliefs around the world, they would need substantial funds. They needed to find a way to fatten their treasury.

Most terrorist organizations are usually funded by private donors. But as ISIS gained more power and more land, the leaders of the group found a new way of financing their terror campaign. As ISIS captured more territory in the oil-rich fields of Iraq and Syria, they sold the oil to fuel its terror machine. They pumped the oil from the ground. They then converted it into fuel oil and

gasoline, using mobile refineries. They shipped these products to the Turkish border and elsewhere. That's where shady merchants and traders bought and sold the oil at a steep discount.

The oil sales provided ISIS with much of its revenue. As a result, experts said ISIS paid its fighters $400 a month, more than the Iraqi army paid its soldiers. In 2015, ISIS had a budget of $2 billion, with a surplus of $250 million. Some of that money went to help disabled people, along with orphans, widows, and families of those killed in the fighting. ISIS had even opened a bank in Mosul, which offered people loans.

Control of oil refining equipment like this in Iraq gave ISIS a steady source of income for its operations.

Knowing how important oil was to ISIS, the United States and other nations began an organized campaign to destroy ISIS' ability to produce oil. By the fall of 2014, the US had destroyed half of the group's refining capabilities. In the process, many engineers and workers were killed or fled.

The operations of ISIS depended on money and information, which Abu Sayyaf was said to control.

Target Abu Sayyaf

Part of the US campaign was to kill or capture Abu Sayyaf. He ran ISIS' financial empire. Unlike Zarqawi and Baghdadi, Sayyaf, whose nickname means "bearer of the sword," was a little-known ISIS leader. (After his capture, US officials said they believed his real name to be Fathi ben Awn ben Jildi Murad al-Tunisi.) Yet, he was a major cog in the group's terrorism machine. Intelligence officials determined that Sayyaf had special knowledge of ISIS' hostage-taking operations. He was also in contact with Baghdadi, whom Sayyaf considered a good friend.

The New York Times had called Sayyaf a "midlevel leader in the organization." Yet, he knew all there was to know about how ISIS worked; how it was funded; and how it conducted its murderous campaign. He had built a network of oil traders and at one point helped triple the amount of money ISIS was bringing in from the illicit oil trade.

Sayyaf found ways to increase production, and, like the head of a corporation, approved ISIS expenses, including how to rebuild damaged oil facilities. Although he was publicly unknown, the members of Delta Force would soon become familiar with Sayyaf and his evil life.

CNN Report

1. MISSION REPORT:
INSIDE DELTA FORCE

It was around noon on April 11, 1980, and President Jimmy Carter had made a bold decision. "Gentlemen," he announced to a meeting of his advisors, "I want you to know that I am seriously considering an attempt to rescue the hostages."

Carter was referring to the 53 Americans held hostage inside the US Embassy in Tehran, the capital of Iran. On November 4, 1979, **militant** Iranian students stormed the walls of the embassy. Once inside, they took 66 Americans captive. By the middle of the month, the Iranians had released 13. Fifty-three, however, remained.

Negotiations proved fruitless. Five months into the crisis, Carter and the American public were desperate for a homecoming. The time, Carter had decided, had come to launch a rescue attempt. The military had been practicing for such an operation for weeks. The mission, code-named Eagle Claw, would be the coming out party of the US Army's newest Special Ops unit, Delta Force.

Words To Understand

counterterrorism activities to fight terrorism

guerrilla a member of a small, independent group that fights larger armies

humanitarian concerned with human health and safety

militant a person who uses violence in support of a political issue

rendezvous meet up at a precise location

During the 1979 Iranian hostage crisis, people in Tehran rallied in support of their national leaders.

The mission was complicated. It called for a nighttime **rendezvous** of helicopters and planes in a desert staging area just south of Tehran. The troops would wait a day. They then planned to move into the Iranian capital, enter the embassy, free the hostages, and bring them out safely.

Army Colonel Charlie Beckwith, who had created Delta Force a few years before, was excited about the mission. He was eager to show off the new force. He would be on the ground in Iran when the mission started.

Debacle in the Desert

Beckwith's men were equally as excited. All had endured a body-bruising selection process. They were ready to jump into action and rescue the

INSIDE DELTA FORCE

A Georgia native, Beckwith played football before joining the army's Green Beret special forces unit.

hostages. Although they were a top-secret force, the men of Delta didn't care that the spotlight would fail to shine on them if the mission was successful. All that mattered was to bring the hostages home.

Beckwith was proud of these men. Most were just as young as the students who had seized the US embassy. The troops had grown long beards for the mission. They also dressed like the students to blend into the Tehran crowd. They wore faded blue jeans and combat boots. Beneath their clothes, they wore armored vests, packed weapons, and tied a rope around their waists.

Beckwith told the president that two small teams had already been in Iran to scout the landing zone, code named Desert One. They found vehicles to carry the raiders to the embassy. Moreover, eight US Navy Stallion helicopters were already in position aboard the *USS Nimitz*, a nuclear-powered aircraft carrier. The helicopters would fly the more than one hundred Delta soldiers into position.

On April 24, the mission began. Things, however, quickly went bad. US forces secured Desert One. They had to hold a busload of civilians that

RH-53D Sea Stallion helicopters like this one were part of the ill-fated Eagle Claw mission to Iran.

Wreckage from the helicopter crash during the failed rescue mission littered the desert.

happened to pass by. The Delta commandos searched the bus for weapons. They found none. Next, two of the eight helicopters from the *Nimitz* experienced mechanical problems. They had to turn back. Moreover, the remaining helicopters arrived at Desert One 90 minutes late. A dust storm then blew up, limiting how far the soldiers and the helicopter and airplane pilots could see. It was now early in the morning on April 25. One of the other copters that had landed was deemed unsafe for the mission.

With only five workable helicopters, commanders decided to abort Operation Eagle Claw. As one of the helicopters attempted to leave, it crashed into a mammoth C-130 airplane. Both exploded in a ball of fire. Eight servicemen died.

Delta Force never got into action. However, the failed mission signaled a drastic change in how US Special Ops forces were to be used in the future. The US Congress investigated the disaster. It found that all the units involved, including those from the US Army, Navy, Air Force, and Marines, were disorganized. Beckwith and others said that all the military's Special Ops forces should be put together in one command, with its own leaders and rules. It would be easier to carry out missions.

Delta Force would have to wait for another day to show off what they could do.

The Worst Kept Secret

Delta Force exists, but not really. It is the newest Special Ops force in the US military, and the most secret. While the Navy SEALs, Army Rangers, and the Green Berets make headlines, Delta Force works mostly without fanfare as an elite **counterterrorism** unit.

Its existence is highly classified, yet it is an open secret. Delta Force has been the focus of books and movies, such as *Black Hawk Down*—a film about a failed **humanitarian** mission in Somalia, a nation in East Africa. Delta Force has been on some high-profile missions, or so rumor has it. Experts say it helped track down the Colombian drug lord Pablo Escobar in 1993. Escobar was killed in a shootout.

At the time Delta Force was formed, the world was a changing place. In the 1960s and 1970s, the Special Forces of the US military, especially those fighting the Vietnam War, focused their attention on secret missions that conventional military forces (tanks, planes, ships, and submarines) could not accomplish.

MISSION REPORT:
INSIDE DELTA FORCE

By the mid-1970s, however, a new type of war was being fought on many fronts. Groups of terrorists believed they could influence political change by attacking civilians. Some hijacked airplanes. Others gunned down tourists. Still others murdered people at nightclubs and restaurants. In 1972, 11 members of the Israeli team were massacred at the Summer Olympic Games in Munich, Germany. The terrorists in that incident were a group of Palestinians known as Black September.

At that time, Beckwith was a Green Beret officer who had fought in Vietnam. He had also spent some time with a British Special Forces unit in the 1960s during a **guerrilla** war in Malaysia. Beckwith left that experience convinced that the US Army needed a similar, elite Special Ops counter-terrorism unit. With the permission of his superiors, Beckwith, along with Colonel Thomas Henry, formed Delta Force. The unit went into operation on November 17, 1977.

The two commanders picked soldiers from the Green Berets and the army's airborne divisions. Each member of the unit had specific skills, such as marksmanship, communication, or tracking. They divided the unit into three combat squadrons, each supported by an intelligence platoon, a signal squad, an aviation platoon, and a support squadron. Each combat unit was nimble enough to be reduced into smaller units.

The technical name for Delta Force is "Special Forces Operation Detachment—Delta." Sometimes Delta Force is called the Combat Applications Group (CAG). The group is based, along with the army Green

Berets, at Fort Bragg, North Carolina. Yet, Delta Force is not an army Special Forces detachment. It is a unit made up of different members of the military. Like other Special Ops, Delta Force can be deployed at a moment's notice.

Delta Force's exploits have spanned the world, from Colombia to Panama, from Afghanistan to Syria. When Iraq invaded its neighbor Kuwait in 1991, Delta Force went behind enemy lines hunting Iraq's Scud missile launchers. Delta Force returned to the Middle East in 2001 after terrorists destroyed the World Trade Center in New York City.

Soldiers like these take on extra training in hopes of being selected to the specialized Delta Force teams.

INSIDE DELTA FORCE

The massive caves and rocky cliffs of Afghanistan's Tora Bora region proved to be good hiding grounds.

The Hunt for Osama Bin Laden

Delta Force and other Special Force units played a major role in the so-called War on Terror. The operation began with the US-led invasion of Afghanistan in October 2001. Delta Force led missions to overthrow the Taliban, the country's fanatical rulers who protected al-Qaeda. Al-Qaeda is the terrorist organization that planned the 9/11 attacks.

As one of its first assignments, Delta Force was given the job of finding al-Qaeda leader Osama bin Laden. Bin Laden was the mastermind of the September 11 attacks. Once US forces arrived in Afghanistan, they determined bin Laden and others were hiding in a cave complex in Tora Bora, southeast of the Afghan capital city Kabul.

Armed with this information, the Delta team was on the march. They drove to the area in several Toyota pickup trucks. The soldiers grew their beards long and wore clothes to match the local Afghans. However, Delta

Force was ordered not to attack the terrorist lair itself. Instead they were told to work closely with the local Afghan forces.

Tora Bora was a valley littered with caves between snow-covered peaks separated by deep streams. Bin Laden's virtually impregnable hideout covered an area roughly six square miles.

Delta Force did not lead the assault on bin Laden's headquarters. Instead, the Afghans took the lead and battled al-Qaeda for two weeks. Delta soldiers established observation posts and called in air strikes by US war planes. When the shooting was over, however, bin Laden had escaped.

The Death of a Drug Kingpin

In the 1980s and early 1990s, a Colombian drug lord named Pablo Escobar was flooding the United States with cocaine, a highly addictive drug. To stop Escobar, the United States deployed Delta Force.

Although its activities remain a secret, the US military's Joint Special Operations Command, the unit responsible for deploying US Special Ops forces, rotated Delta Force and the US Navy SEAL Team 6, into and out of Colombia in the search for Escobar. On December 2, 1993, Escobar was killed by Colombian authorities during a raid in his hometown. Many suspect Delta Force had played a major role.

CARCEL OTTO JUDICIAL
MEDELLIN

128482

INSIDE DELTA FORCE

Operation Urgent Fury

It had been nearly three years since Delta Force and other Special Ops units were left flatfooted in the Iranian desert during Operation Eagle Claw. Finally, on October 25, 1983, Delta Force was put into action during the US-invasion of Grenada—Operation Urgent Fury.

Grenada was a small island in the Caribbean, home to nearly 1,000 Americans, many of them students at the island's medical school. In 1983, a group of communists, those who believe in a planned society, violently took control of the government. Many of Grenada's residents became angry and

An army helicopter lands on the Caribbean island of Grenada during the 1983 mission to rescue students.

protested the new government. Violence erupted. As the fighting escalated, US President Ronald Reagan feared the Americans were in danger. He became even more concerned after the new Grenadian government said that no Americans could leave the island.

The Americans were now prisoners. In response, Reagan ordered the US military to invade and bring the Americans home. Nearly 2,000 troops landed on the island. They faced opposition not only from Grenada's small army, but from groups of Cuban soldiers as well.

Part of the invasion called for a platoon of Delta Force commandos to fly into the country before the invasion. Its mission was to clear out Fort Rupert—home of the Revolutionary Council, the island-nation's new government. The Deltas (with a Ranger battalion) were then to rescue political prisoners at the Richmond Hill Prison. The area was heavily defended as the troopers flew over the area in a helicopter. The Grenadian and Cuban forces immediately fired on the Delta platoon and the Rangers and the mission had to be aborted. The invasion had been successful, however, and the Americans were brought home.

Training for Delta Force

As with all Special Ops units in the US military, the soldiers of Delta Force undergo difficult physical and mental training. Delta Force recruits some of its members from other Special Force units, including the Army Rangers. The selection process takes nearly a month.

MISSION REPORT:
INSIDE DELTA FORCE

Before becoming a Delta Force commando, recruits undertake a series of physical and mental tests to determine whether they can handle the job. Training is based on the British special ops unit that Colonel Beckwith served with prior to his forming the Delta unit.

These soldiers carry heavy packs during army training, similar to the long marches undertaken in Delta preparations.

The Night Stalkers

When Delta Force units need to fly into a situation without being noticed, they rely on the Night Stalkers, a group of highly trained pilots in the 160th Special Operations Aviation Regiment. Piloting Black Hawk and Little Bird helicopters, the Night Stalkers travel close to the ground to insert Delta Force operators as close to the target as possible.

Delta recruits must know how to navigate using maps and compasses. As they train, the recruits carry heavy rucksacks. One test involves marching 18 miles (28 km) at night with 35 pounds (15 kg) of gear. Another is a timed 40-mile (64-km) march over rough terrain carrying 45 pounds (20 kg).

Those who pass the selection process, enter the six-month Operators Training Course, or OTC. Here, among other things, the soldiers learn how to become snipers. They learn how to clear rooms of hostages and enemy targets. They learn how to pick locks and make bombs. They practice all types of rescue scenarios. They also learn how set up sniper positions and various spying techniques.

The Delta Force training facility is known as the "House of Horrors." Because each combat situation is different, the trainees sharpen their skills practicing in buses, trains, and passenger planes.

Training video

2. PREPARING FOR ACTION

The members of Delta Force served with distinction against al-Qaeda and the Taliban in Afghanistan. On March 24, 2003, a new mission began—the invasion of Iraq. One of Delta's first assignments was to go behind enemy lines to scout out the Haditha Dam. Once they got settled, the Delta unit then called in airstrikes on several targets. It also provided critical intelligence on the Iraqis protecting the dam, resulting in the facility's capture.

Delta Force was also **instrumental** during several major battles during the war, including the First Battle of Fallujah in 2004. Delta Force also participated in several rescue missions, including one in which the unit rescued several Italian and Polish security contractors. When the fighting shifted to Syria years later, Delta Force was ready.

Words To Understand

coalition an alliance between countries

informants spies

instrumental helpful

operatives expert workers hired for a specific task

US Army units patrol the beach near the vital Iraqi target of the Haditha Dam, where Delta worked in 2003.

ISIS and the Syrian Civil War

In March 2011, pro-democracy protesters staged uprisings in the southern Syrian city of Deraa. The protests began after the government of President Bashar al-Assad arrested and tortured teenagers who had painted anti-government slogans on a school wall.

The arrests spawned a series of demonstrations. People called for al-Assad to step down. In response, al-Assad ordered the military to crush the protests. Violence ultimately raged throughout the summer. It escalated into a bloody civil war between Syria's majority Sunni population and al-Assad's ruling minority Shiite government.

ISIS took advantage of the conflict to strengthen its ranks. The conflict began to spiral out of control as the United States and other nations gradually became involved. By the summer of 2015, some 250,000 Syrians had been killed as the Islamic State began building its caliphate in Syria and Iraq. ISIS fought against al-Assad's government. ISIS quickly captured major cities, such as Raqqa and Deir ez-Zor. ISIS then raced across Iraq and captured Mosul.

Syria became a problem for the United States. The US wanted al-Assad, a brutal dictator, out of power. As a result, it began to supply the rebels with food and other non-military equipment. The US also turned its attention on fighting ISIS. The group had been responsible for unspeakable atrocities in

Refugees from Syria had to live in camps such as this one when fighting in their homeland forced them to flee.

US forces bombed ISIS targets inside Syria in 2015 in an attempt to drive out the invading forces.

Iraq and Syria. It was also killing innocent civilians, journalists, and members of Christian minority groups in Iraq and Syria. ISIS had staged or supported several deadly terror attacks around the world.

Hoping to stop the bloodshed, President Obama ordered the US military to bomb ISIS targets. Obama said the goal was to create "a steady, relentless effort to take out [ISIL] wherever they exist." Obama also put together a **coalition** of governments to fight the group.

Central to the Fight

Delta Force was central to destroying ISIS in Syria and Iraq. The mission was called Operation Inherent Resolve. Delta Force immediately began setting up

The high-speed Night Hawk helicopter has played vital roles in inserting Delta Force teams to hot spots.

safe houses and building a network of **informants** that could give them information on killing or capturing ISIS **operatives**.

On July 4, 2014, for example, the Night Stalkers flew 24 Delta Force commandos into Syria to find a group of American hostages, including journalist James Foley. Although the hostages were not present at the ISIS base, Delta Force killed several ISIS fighters.

Delta Force used the same strategy in Syria that Special Operations forces used for years in Iraq and Afghanistan. The Delta Force plan was to gather as much intelligence as it could, and then stage raids on ISIS bases and hideouts. Not only were Delta teams to kill and capture terrorists, but they would also look for laptops, cell phones, and other intelligence to understand how the terrorist network ran and who else might be involved.

In the meantime, the United States was waging war against ISIS on another front—stopping the flow of money. Not only did the Americans want to destroy ISIS bases, but to disrupt the flow of oil that financed the group as well.

"As commander in chief, my highest priority is the security of the American people," Obama said. "Over the last several years, we have consistently taken the fight to terrorists who threaten our country…Thanks to our military and counterterrorism professionals, America is safer… I will not hesitate to take action against [ISIS] in Syria, as well as Iraq. This is a core principle of my presidency: if you threaten America, you will find no safe haven."

Those words would soon ring true for Abu Sayyaf.

President Barack Obama ordered US forces to assist people in Syria who were fighting against ISIS.

A Hostage

Abu Sayyaf was a fake name. His real name was Fathi ben Awn ben Jildi Murad al-Tunisi. He was born in Tunis, Algeria. Sayyaf not only ran the finances of ISIS, but he and his wife, Umm Sayyaf, also known as Nisreen Assad Ibrahim Bahar, were suspected of holding an American aid worker hostage. Her name was Kayla Mueller.

Mueller, 26, from Prescott, Arizona, saw what was happening in Syria and wanted to do something. Her heart ached for the children of that war-torn

Doctors Without Borders is an international medical aid group that focuses on helping refugees and disaster victims.

country, and the tens of thousands of refugees who tried to find a safe place to live among the bombed-out buildings and rubble of their cities.

In December 2012, Mueller decided to travel to Turkey and help the thousands of Syrian refugees who were pouring into that country. "For as long as I live, I will not let this suffering be normal," she told an

Death of Mueller

Arizona newspaper. Mueller traveled to the city of Antakya, which was only a half-hour drive from the Syrian border.

On Aug. 3, 2013, Mueller and a friend who worked for Doctors Without Borders traveled to the Syrian city of Aleppo to help install a communications system at a hospital. They spent the night at the hospital and headed back to Turkey the next day. It was then that ISIS fighters took Mueller, her friend, and two others hostage. All but Mueller were eventually released.

For 18 months, Mueller was held against her will. Part of that time she was a prisoner of Abu Sayyaf and his wife. They had kept the American as a slave for ISIS leader Abu Bakr al-Baghdadi. US officials have said that Umm Sayyaf was the "sole" person responsible for Mueller while in captivity. Umm Sayyaf would threaten Mueller and other hostages, threatening to kill them if they did not listen to her.

3. MISSION REPORT:
GEAR UP

D elta Force is so elite that is has a wide array of weapons at its disposal, or so many people believe. Some of these weapons are customized, or made specially, for Delta Force.

HK416 and PSG1

Delta Force is thought to use the HK416 carbine, which is a light automatic rifle. The weapon was designed specifically for Delta Force by the German arms manufacturer, Heckler and Koch (HK). The company also makes the PSG1, a semiautomatic sniper rifle. It is said that the company designed the PSG1 after the Munich massacre at the 1972 Olympic Games. The West German police could not engage the terrorists quickly enough and wanted a new weapon to help them. The range of the PSG1 is 2,625 feet (800 m) and is fed by a 20-round magazine.

Browning M82A1

Sometimes a Delta Force mission calls for a larger sniper rifle. To that end, the M82A1 is a portable semiautomatic .50-caliber rifle that can hold up to 10 rounds of ammunition. The rifle was used by American soldiers during Operation Desert Shield in 1991. Its incredibly long range, roughly 1.1 miles (1.7 km), makes it the weapon of choice when scoping out such targets as parked aircraft and radar huts.

Delta Force used the M82A1 to disable a prison generator in Panama during the rescue of Kurt Muse in 1989. Muse was reportedly an operative

The Colt M4 is the standard rifle used by Delta Force operatives. The gun is both lightweight and durable.

for the Central Intelligence Agency, who was jailed in the country's notorious prison, Carcel Modelo. The Delta team rescued Muse.

Colt M4

This carbine has a short barrel and is easy to use in close quarters. The M4 is classified by its maker as a submachine, a portable automatic machine gun that can be fired from the shoulder or hip. A Delta Force sniper named Gary Gordon used a M4 when he defended a Black Hawk helicopter that had been shot down in Mogadishu, Somalia, in 1993.

Little Bird

Experts say Delta Force relies on its own aviation platoon to get them in and out of certain missions. The platoon operates a small fleet of helicopters that look like civilian aircraft. Among them is the MH-6 Little Bird. Built by the aircraft company Boeing, the Little Bird is a light helicopter designed to carry up to six commandos. The AH-6 is a gunship version of this helicopter.

Chinook and Black Hawk Helicopters

The Delta Force aviation platoon should not be confused with the Night Stalkers, although the Night Stalkers do have the Little Birds in their arsenal. The Night Stalkers can shuttle Delta Force commandos to and from their missions using a variety of helicopters. The Night Stalkers use the MH-47G Chinook and the MH-60 Black Hawk.

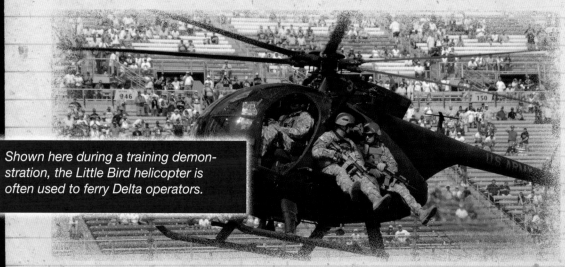

Shown here during a training demonstration, the Little Bird helicopter is often used to ferry Delta operators.

The larger Black Hawk helicopter can haul in gear and personnel, or hover to extract fighters from the ground.

Both helicopters are well known in the world of Special Ops. The Black Hawk is an assault helicopter that can be used to drop and remove personnel into and out of combat. It is equipped with a rope that is lowered down to the ground. On the rope is a series of rings. The rings allow commandos wearing special harnesses to hook onto the rope and be pulled to safety. Eight troops in full combat gear can be pulled out of a mission and spirited away at one time using this method.

The Chinook is much larger and has two rotors. Special Op forces use the Chinook during heavy assault missions and resupply operations. Among other things, the various Chinook models come equipped with an early warning missile system; a laser warning system, and high frequency radios, whose signal cannot be jammed by the enemy.

4. DELTA FORCE GOES IN

The Kurds are the fourth-largest ethnic group in the Middle East. There are between 25 and 35 million living in the region. Although they do not have a country of their own, the Kurds live in a mountainous region spanning the borders of Turkey, Iraq, Syria, Iran, and Armenia. Although most Kurds are Sunni Muslims, many practice different religions.

In 2013, ISIS began attacking several Kurdish communities in territory the terrorist group held in northern Syria. The attacks continued for a year, until ISIS began its invasion of Iraq in June 2014. As ISIS advanced toward Mosul and other Iraqi cities, the Iraqi army melted away. As a result, the Kurds were forced to battle the group to protect their homes.

The fighting was rough. ISIS halted the advance on Kurdish territory in Iraq. Yet, the group still tried to capture Kurdish territory in Syria. Tens of thousands of Kurds were left bruised and bloody by the violence. They left their homes and sought safety in Turkey as **refugees**. The Kurds were the sworn enemy of ISIS. They would play an important role in bringing down Abu Sayyaf.

Words To Understand

deploy move military forces to strategic locations

refugees people who are forced to leave their homes because of war, natural disasters, or some other calamity

Dedicated men and women fight to defend Kurdish territory from advancing ISIS forces in Iraq.

A Special Relationship

For decades, the Central Intelligence Agency (CIA), the spy agency of the United States, had a special relationship with the Kurds. In 1992, for example, Kurds joined a CIA-backed rebel army that was battling Saddam Hussein's military. When the United States invaded Iraq in 2003, Kurds living in the northern part of the country could not have been happier. Hussein had tried to destroy the Kurds years before. He even used chemical weapons against them. While many people around the world considered the US-led military

Kurdish forces celebrated after capturing a tank during a battle against ISIS and other anti-Kurdish people.

action an "invasion," the Kurds called it a "liberation." The CIA worked closely with the Kurds to defeat Hussein's army.

This special relationship continued well into 2015, when the US was poised to take out Abu Sayyaf. At that time, Sayyaf was hiding out in the town of al-Amr in eastern Syria, deep in ISIS territory. Kurdish forces living near the town reported back to the CIA about what they knew and what they saw. They pinpointed the exact location of Sayyaf's hideout. Moreover, the Kurdish spies said, Sayyaf and his wife were holding hostage several young women as slaves for ISIS leaders.

Armed with this information, President Barack Obama and his military and civilian advisors decided the time had come to go after Sayyaf. Yet, they weren't ready to launch an attack. The president needed more information. The US turned to Delta Force and the British for help.

British Special Ops

With approval from the White House and Pentagon, US commanders asked Great Britain's elite Special Operations force, Special Air Service (SAS), to

As in many cases of special forces images, faces of SAS soldiers are blurred to protect their identity.

Medal for a Delta

In 2012, Master Sergeant David R. Halbruner, won the Distinguished Service Cross as Delta Force tried to rescue US diplomats who were under attack at the US mission in Benghazi, Libya.

Although Delta Force's role in trying to rescue the diplomats and others is a secret, the army says Halbruner was one of seven US military personnel who went to Benghazi on the night of September 11, 2012. At that time, terrorists stormed the consulate, killing US Ambassador J. Christopher Stevens and Sean Smith, an employee of the US State Department.

Halbruner and the others chartered a plane in Tripoli when the attack began and made their way to the consulate. The army does not name Halbruner's unit. He was only described as "a team leader for a joint task force in support of an overseas contingency operation."

Halbruner's citation reads in part: "Without regard for his own safety, Master Sergeant Halbruner's valorous actions, dedication to duty and willingness to place himself in harm's way for the protection of others was critical to the success of saving numerous United States civilian lives. Throughout the operation, Master Sergeant Halbruner continually exposed himself to fire as he shepherded unarmed civilians to safety and treated the critically wounded. His calm demeanor, professionalism and courage was an inspiration to all and contributed directly to the success of the mission. Master Sergeant Halbruner's distinctive accomplishments are in keeping with the finest traditions of the military service and reflect great credit upon himself, his Command and the United States Army."

participate in the raid. Formed in 1941 at the height of World War II (1939–1945), SAS commandos specialized in hostage rescue, secret reconnaissance, and counterterrorism.

The SAS proved its worth as ISIS grew in power and territory. Although they wouldn't go into actual combat, the British military decided to **deploy** SAS in both Iraq and Syria. SAS trained and advised the Iraqi army and Kurdish fighters. When the Americans called, SAS did not flinch. Special Air Service troops joined the American-led mission. The plan to capture or kill Abu Sayyaf was as straightforward as it was complicated. To keep their involvement a secret, SAS troops shed their British uniforms and suited up as US soldiers. They even carried the same assault rifles as Delta Force.

Digging In

The mission, however, had to be called off twice—once because of problems with equipment and again because of bad weather. Finally, everything fell into place and on the third attempt the mission was a go. Dozens of SAS commandos climbed aboard Osprey aircraft and landed just outside what the Americans believed was Sayyaf's hideout. There, in the scorching heat of the Syrian desert, SAS soldiers dug in to provide critical reconnaissance on Sayyaf's whereabouts.

The SAS were armed with sophisticated high-resolution cameras with telescopic lens. They trained these high-powered lenses on the compound surrounded by ISIS fighters.

The SAS took detailed pictures of the enemy fighters and sent them back to US commanders at the US Central Command based in the nation of Qatar. Obama wanted to make sure that Sayyaf was at the compound before ordering Delta Force into battle. Only when the SAS provided the Americans with that information did Obama and his commanders make the final decision to attack.

Jets help the Osprey aircraft rise like a helicopter. The devices then rotate to let the propellers drive the Osprey forward.

One of the hardest hit groups in the Middle East was the Yazidi people, who were driven from their homes en masse.

Early Morning Raid

The early morning hours of May 16, 2015, were as dark as it gets in the desert. Fast asleep in a room of Sayyaf's hideout was a teenage girl. She was a Yazidi, a member of a small Kurdish religious group who called northern Iraq, southeastern Turkey, and northern Syria home. The girl had days earlier been taken hostage by Sayyaf. At around 2 AM the attack began. The girl looked up as she heard several US jets scream overhead. As they passed the compound, the pilots fired their weapons, mowing down ISIS fighters with rockets and machine-gun fire.

The young prisoner listened and cowered for safety. In another room Sayyaf, his wife, her sister and brother-in-law, who was Sayyaf's bodyguard, ducked for cover in fear as the jets flew above. Soon after, the jets roared away, and in the sparse silence came the heavily armed members of Delta Force.

Black Hawk helicopters and an Osprey tilt-rotor aircraft carrying Delta Force and SAS personnel landed near the multi-storied building. The aircraft were flown by the Night Stalkers and pilots from the Air Force Special Operations Command.

As the troops landed, they came under heavy fire from a group of ISIS fighters. The battle was on. At different points, Delta Force fought hand-to-hand with the terrorists. As they fought, the Delta troops rushed inside the building. They then smashed through the front door, killing one of Sayyaf's bodyguards standing on a set of stairs. As Delta Force commandos made their way deeper into the house, SAS personnel formed a ring around the compound to stop any ISIS fighter from escaping alive.

'I am a Yazidi Girl'

As Delta Force stormed up the stairs, Sayyaf and his wife ran to the hostage's room. They grabbed the girl and attempted to escape with her. As the three ran down a hall, Sayyaf came upon the US troops. The Americans aimed their automatic rifles at the ISIS leader. Sayyaf reached for his gun. The Americans fired two shots into his chest. Sayyaf, bearded and tall, fell backwards on the floor. He was dead.

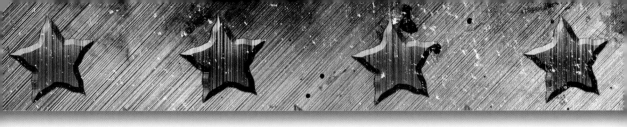

The Delta Force commandos asked the girl who she was. "I am a Yazidi girl who has been captured," she said. She explained that she had been kidnapped about seven months before in Mosul. She was eventually sold to Sayyaf.

Sayyaf's wife, wracked with fear, blurted out in a lie: "I am also a Yazidi." But the young girl was now safe. She told the Americans who the woman was. They put handcuffs on Umm Sayyaf and led her away.

Delta Force operators train constantly, practicing just about any situation they might find themselves in.

Vital Intel

Sayyaf was dead, but the mission was not over. Delta Force went from room to room looking for any intelligence they could find. The troops weren't disappointed. They found several laptop computers and cell phones, all of which contained valuable intelligence.

With the Yazidi girl and Sayyaf's wife in tow, the time had come for Delta Force to leave the area. Outside, several ISIS fighters remained. The troopers ordered the women to stay close to them as the Americans and British engaged the terrorists.

One of the best ways to get enemy information is to capture laptops, cell phones, and computer disks.

Delta Force operatives often rappel down from hovering helicopters to reach targets on the ground.

Corpses of ISIS fighters (no Americans or British soldiers were killed during the fight) littered the sand as two Black Hawk helicopters swooped in to pick up the commandos. The women and the troops were whisked away to a US airbase in northern Iraq.

A Story to Tell

Now that she was in the hands of the Americans, the teenage girl had a story to tell the Kurdish and US intelligence officers. She had been captured in August 2014 when ISIS fighters overran her Yazidi village. She said Sayyaf had

Shrouded in mystery, their identities a secret, Delta Force operators remain ever vigilant to act when called.

bought her only a few weeks before the raid. During that time, he beat her terribly. She also told the investigators that Sayyaf had imprisoned Kayla Mueller at a different house. She was kept there under orders of Sayyaf's "best friend," al-Baghdadi, the head of the terrorist group. Mueller died in Syria in 2015.

Mission Accomplished

The raid on Sayyaf's compound was the first successful raid inside ISIS territory by the United States. It underscored the importance of the CIA's Kurdish spy network. Other raids would soon follow.

Back in Washington, Obama and his team were very pleased that the raid had gone well. The US did not coordinate the attack with the Syrian government, nor did they tell it what was going to happen.

"Abu Sayyaf was a senior ISIL leader who, among other things, had a senior role in overseeing ISIL's illicit oil and gas operations—a key source of revenue that enables the terrorist organization to carry out their brutal tactics and oppress thousands of innocent civilians," National Security Council spokeswoman Bernadette Meehan said in a statement after the raid. "He was also involved with the group's military operations."

Delta Force stood down to await its next mission.

ABC News on mission

TEXT-DEPENDENT QUESTIONS

1. What is a caliphate?

2. How did ISIS make money to finance its terror campaign?

3. When was Delta Force first formed?

4. What was Operation Eagle Claw and what was its outcome?

5. Who are the "Night Stalkers"?

6. Which Special Ops unit fought with Delta Force during the raid on Abu Sayyaf's compound in Syria?

RESEARCH PROJECTS

1. Read more about the Iranian hostage crisis of 1979. Create a timeline of events, starting with the hostage-taking and ending with their release.

2. Read more about the Yazidi people and their plight. What has happened to them? Where have they been forced to move? Find five organizations that are working to help them.

3. Look online to find the Delta Force application requirements. What are they? What sort of people do you think would make good Delta Force operators? As of 2017, women were not allowed to be in Delta Force. Write a pros and cons sheet showing why that is or is not a good idea.

4. Research other Delta Force missions. You'll find that there are not many that have been declassified. See if you can find enough about one to give a short report on the reasons for the mission and its outcome.

FIND OUT MORE

Websites

Military.com Delta Force

http://www.military.com/special-operations/delta-force.html

Lockheed Martin: Black Hawk Helicopter

http://lockheedmartin.com/us/products/h-60-black-hawk-helicopter.html

ISIS Fast Facts: CNN

http://www.cnn.com/2014/08/08/world/isis-fast-facts/

Books

Beckwith, Charlie, and Donald Knox. *Delta Force: A Memoir by the Founder of the Military's Most Secretive Special-Operations Unit.* New York: William Morrow, 2013.

Haney, Eric. *Inside Delta Force: The Story of America's Elite Counterterrorism Unit.* New York: Delacorte Books, 2006.

Pushies, Fred. *Weapons of Delta Force.* St. Paul, MN: MBI Publishing, 2012.

Ryan, Mike. *The Operators: Inside the World's Special Forces.* Amazon (Kindle Edition), 2014.

SERIES GLOSSARY OF KEY TERMS

coalition a group of allies working toward a similar goal

commando a highly trained soldier in a special operations force

counterterrorism efforts to prevent terrorist attacks and arrest the people who plan and carry them out

diversionary an action designed to redirect somebody's attention away from something

encrypted protected by a code or software that prevents someone from accessing computer data

guerrilla irregular or surprise methods of fighting, often by small groups

ideological based on a system of ideals and ideas, usually concerning economics or politics

intelligence secretly gathered information about an enemy

operatives expert workers hired for a specific task

paramilitary organized similarly to a military force

propaganda information put forth by a group to promote an idea or policy

reconnaissance surveying an area to collect strategic information about it

rendezvous meet up at a precise location

terrorist person who uses violence for political purposes

INDEX

PHOTO CREDITS

ABOUT THE AUTHOR

John Perritano is an award-winning journalist, writer, and editor from Southbury, Connecticut, who has written numerous articles and books on a variety of subjects, including science, sports, history, and culture for such publishers as National Geographic, Scholastic, and Time/Life. His articles have appeared on Discovery.com, Popular Mechanics.com, and other magazines and websites. He holds a master's degree in American History from Western Connecticut State University.